contents

the Saxon Shore Way

Imagine stepping back in time and discovering the coastline of the Garden of England as it stood more than 1,600 years ago – the end of the Roman Empire and the beginning of the Dark Ages.

Explore the remains of once-thriving ports with access to mainland Europe and beyond. Discover the castles and fortifications built to keep less welcome visitors at bay.

The Saxon Shore Way is more than160 miles (257km) of some of the finest coastal walking in England. The paths cross two Areas of Outstanding Natural Beauty and numerous Sites of Special Scientific Interest. There are dramatic changes in landscape from the spectacular White Cliffs at Dover to the mysterious and haunting levels of Romney Marsh.

The Saxon Shore Way is a waymarked network of ancient and modern paths and tracks running from Gravesend in north Kent through to Hastings, East Sussex. Kent County Council first established the route in 1980.

Hundreds of enthusiastic walkers have now completed the full length of the Saxon Shore Way. Many more enjoy returning time and again to spend a few hours tracing the ancient shoreline through nature reserves, busy ports, popular seaside resorts, picturesque market towns and traditional Kent orchards.

This guidebook provides an overview of the many walking experiences to be savoured along the Saxon Shore Way. The guide also includes details and maps of eight short, circular walks as an introduction to the many different landscapes just waiting to be explored.

St Margaret's Bay

5

"The world, according to the best geographers, is divided into Europe, Asia, Africa, America, and Romney Marsh"
(from Ingoldsby Legends, the Reverend Richard Harris Barham)

6

"*The sum of the whole is this: walk and be happy; walk and be healthy. The best way to lengthen out our days is to walk steadily and with a purpose.*"
(Charles Dickens)

View from Lympne

time & tide

The Saxon Shore Way is named after the line of fortifications defending the Kent coast at the end of the Roman era. In the *Notitia Dignitatum* (a list of all troop postings across the Roman Empire), there is a reference to a Count of the Saxon Shore.

The remains of many of these forts and Roman defences, such as Stutfall Castle (Portus Lemanis), near Lympne, stand many miles from the current coastline (see Walk 6). They rest on cliffs marooned in fields overlooking miles of arable and grazing pasture rather than the sea. Others, like Reculver, have almost slipped away into the sea entirely.

Meanwhile, long-standing key defences, such as Dover Castle, still command their original imposing positions towering above the English Channel (see Walk 5).

The coastline of Kent has changed dramatically over the centuries as the result of natural processes, such as marine erosion, and the intervention of people seeking more land for their crops and herds.

For example, the Romney and Walland marshes began to form as silt brought down by the River Rother combined with a steady drift of pebbles along the Channel coast from west to east. Local people then constructed a network of ditches and dykes to drain the land to create arable land and pasture.

Drainage of the current stretch of Romney Marsh was virtually completed by the 17th century (see Walk 8). From the 11th century, a similar process of "inning" with the aid of wattle fences created much of the current North Kent marshlands.

During the Roman period, the Isle of Thanet was separated from the mainland by the Wantsum Channel – a tidal channel more than a third of a mile wide (500m) bordered by salt marshes covered by water at high tide.

Mud deposits gradually built up narrowing the channel, which had been an excellent route for traders moving goods and vessels between the English Channel and the Greater Thames Estuary. People began to reclaim the marshland by building barriers to keep the sea out and digging ditches to drain the land (see Walk 3).

Reculver

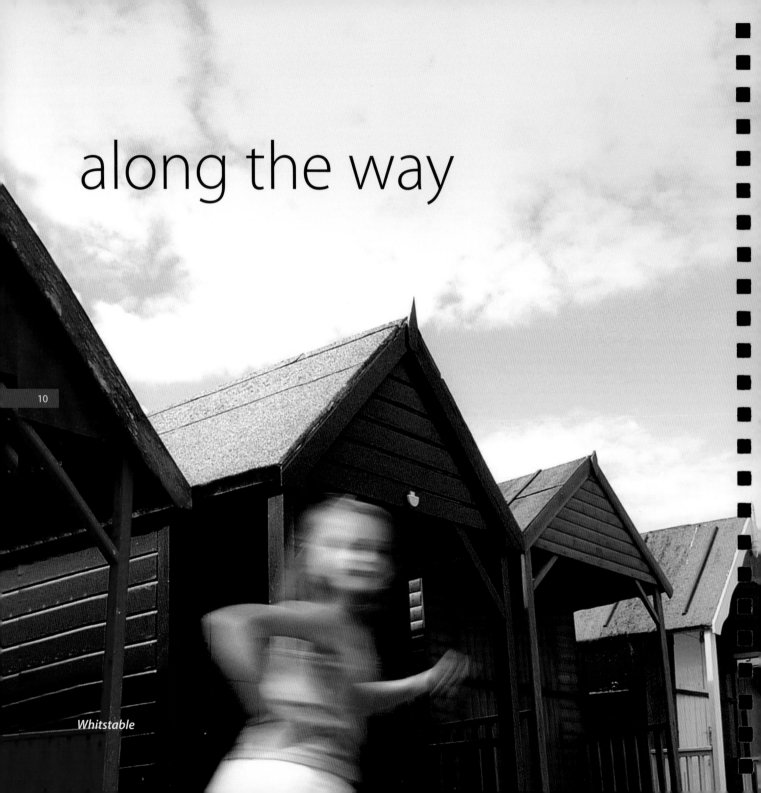

along the way

10

Whitstable

From the bustling port of Gravesend on the River Thames to the seaside resort of Hastings, the Saxon Shore Way passes through many thriving towns and villages.

Leaving Gravesend, the path heads off towards the Hoo peninsula and on towards the Medway towns of Rochester, Chatham and Gillingham closely followed by Sittingbourne and Faversham.

From the creeks and riverside marshes, the route proceeds along the Kent coast. Whitstable and Herne Bay offer a wealth of opportunities for entertainment and rest before turning inland to follow what was once the shoreline of the Wantsum Channel. The path then heads towards the ancient port of Sandwich, the Roman fortifications at Richborough and the fishing town of Deal.

Back on the coast, the Saxon Shore Way gradually rises, with spectacular views over The English Channel, to the White Cliffs and the busy harbour and cruise terminal at Dover.

After Folkestone, the path leads to the North Downs and the Greensand Ridge taking in an overview of the most recent trading link with mainland Europe – the Channel Tunnel – and the Roman port at Lympne.

The old shoreline above Romney Marsh eventually joins the banks of the River Rother to arrive at Rye with its fine medieval and Georgian buildings.

From Rye, following first the River Brede and then the Royal Military Canal, the Saxon Shore Way skirts the edge of the Weald past Winchelsea and through to Hastings Country Park with distant views of Beachy Head.

Finally, the path drops steeply down the sandstone cliffs to return to sea level and opportunities to explore the Old Town of Hastings.

The eight walks in this guidebook have been selected to give a "taste" of the many different landscapes to be discovered along the Saxon Shore Way in Kent.

Dover Castle

frontlines & foreshores

Over the centuries, Kent – the gateway to mainland Europe and the rest of the world – has seen its people prosper from the many trading links and political relationships it has forged overseas. However, these strengths, boosted by the county's routes to London, have also been seen as its greatest weakness.

Each key stage in the history of England has left its imprint along the coastline of this county. From the arrival of the Romans to the earliest Saxon Kingdom and the Norman Conquest, through the Napoleonic Wars, the growth of the British Empire and the two world wars.

Kent has always been at the frontline – either defending the nation against invaders or welcoming early Christian evangelists such as Augustine.

The remnants of the response to past threats can be found right along the coast, the River Medway

and The Thames. These range from Iron Age hill forts, Roman fortresses, Medieval and Tudor castles and Martello towers to a fortified canal and concrete pill boxes.

The Confederation of the Cinque Ports – originally the five towns of Hastings, Romney, Hythe, Sandwich and Dover – worked for 500 years to provide the Kings and Queens of England with ships and men to watch the English Channel and transport soldiers to the Continent.

The Royal Dockyard, at Chatham, which had a long tradition of building warships before the

Spanish Armada and saw the launch of HMS Victory in 1765, grew to meet the needs of the Navy. Chatham Historic Dockyard is now open to the public.

Fortifications and plans to deter potential invasions during the Napoleonic Wars can be found along the current and former coastline and include the Royal Military Canal.

One of only two wholly state-funded canals constructed in Britain, the Royal Military Canal was never called upon to prove its worth as a defence. It now contributes to the drainage of Romney Marsh and is a Scheduled Monument.

Castle enthusiasts will find a wealth of examples along the Saxon Shore Way. The first after leaving Gravesend, is Cooling Castle, a fortified manor house built in 1381. Nearby, Upnor Castle was built in the 1560s to protect the Royal Navy anchored in the Medway. Upnor did not see action until the Dutch fleet made a daring raid up the river more than a century later.

Defence of the river was also key for the Norman castle at Rochester with its fine ragstone tower. Sandown Castle, Deal Castle and Walmer Castle were built as a group by Henry VIII to defend the English Channel. Walmer is now the official residence of the Lord Warden of the Cinque Ports.

Dover Castle, with its Norman stone walls, is undoubtedly the most famous castle along the Saxon Shore Way not least because of its magnificent position perched on top of the majestic White Cliffs. Saltwood Castle stands alone as the only castle built for the Archbishop of Canterbury. Camber Castle, on the final stretch of the Saxon Shore Way, was also commissioned by Henry VIII to defend against the French. The building was finally completed in 1540 and is now situated inland in an area of important wildlife.

To find out more about some of these fortifications visit www.fortifications.org

naturally inspiring

There are unique environments and habitats each with their own populations of plants and animals right along the Saxon Shore Way. Every walker will return with their own special memories.

There are numerous Sites of Special Scientific Interest (SSSI) and National Nature Reserves. And the North Kent Marshes are recognised as one of the most important estuarine habitats for birds in the UK. These are outstanding places to visit to admire flocks of migrating birds, wildfowl and wading birds, plants, butterflies and moths, invertebrates and small mammals.

The sheer beauty and atmosphere of the Kent coast has inspired such artists as J. M. W. Turner and W.L.Wylie as well as numerous writers. Joseph Conrad provides a memorable description of the Thames, at Gravesend, in Heart of Darkness. Charles Dickens draws on the mists of the marshes for scenes in Great Expectations as well as many other Kent locations in his other novels. And the chalk cliffs at Dover set the backdrop for dramatic scenes in Shakespeare's King Lear. Numerous other writers have chosen to locate their tales amid the mysteries of Romney Marsh.

Further details of nature reserves and country parks on or near the Saxon Shore Way are available at www.kent.gov.uk/explorekent

a fresh approach to keeping fit

Walking is one of the most pleasurable ways to improve your health, enhance stamina and energy, lower blood pressure and reduce stress.

In addition to the Saxon Shore Way, Kent has a vast range of rural, coastal and town centre walks to suit walkers of all ages and abilities.

As walking requires very little equipment and can be enjoyed throughout the year on your own or with family and friends, it must surely be the most cost-effective and fun way to keep fit.

Ten thousands steps a day are recommended for a healthy lifestyle. Visit www.kent.gov.uk/explorekent for more information.

Please consult your doctor when undertaking any new physical exercise.

planning your walk

Make sure you have appropriate maps and information about the walk you are planning.

Make a good estimate of how long the walk is likely to take you. Most people average 2 miles (3 kilometres) an hour – steep slopes and rough ground can make the going much slower.

Remember to allow time for rests, refreshment breaks and simply savouring the views.
If you are not used to walking, start with a short walk of 1.5 – 2 miles (2–3 km) see Walk 7 or 8.

Check the weather forecast for the day. Wear loose-fitting, comfortable and bright clothing appropriate for the season and road walking. Select strong, comfortable shoes with a good gripping sole or walking boots. Sun cream is always advisable but particularly during the spring and summer.

Drink plenty of water and take snacks with you.

Carry a mobile phone and let someone else know where you are going and when you expect to return.

If your walk takes you along roads, or across roads, please take care and follow the Highway Code (www.highwaycode.gov.uk).

Signage on Public Rights of Way

Where footpaths, bridleways or byways join a road, a right of way sign (see below) will indicate the route to follow. Additionally, to help people follow a route, waymarkers are installed along a right of way. These are usually coloured arrows fixed or painted onto stiles and gateposts (see below).

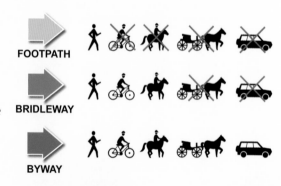

FOOTPATH

BRIDLEWAY

BYWAY

Signpost   Waymarker

The Countryside Code
Respect – Protect – Enjoy

If you follow the Countryside Code wherever you go, you will enjoy walking in Kent and help protect the countryside now and for future generations.

Be safe, plan ahead and follow any signs. Leave gates and property as you find them.
Protect plants and animals, and take your litter home. Keep dogs under close control.
Consider other people.

Dog walking

The countryside is a great place for dogs to enjoy whether ambling along leafy lanes, rambling through forests, or exploring open access land.

This sign identifies walks in this guidebook that are considered particularly appropriate for dogs.

For further information about the Countryside Code, or copies of "You and your dog in the countryside", visit **www.countrysideacess.gov.uk** or phone **0845 100 3298**.

get walking

The following eight circular walks are an excellent introduction to the different landscapes and environments to be enjoyed along the Saxon Shore Way.

Each walk is easy to find with the help of a road map or you can choose to travel by public transport. You will also find information about where to park, the type and length of the walk and where to enjoy a well earned rest.

Rochester, Sandwich and Hamstreet can all be explored directly from a nearby railway station. So, for the walks in these areas, you can leave your car at home and catch the train.

There are a selection of interesting facts about local history and the many places to be discovered on your walks and nearby. The paths are clearly marked with references to Ordnance Survey Explorer map numbers to help walkers planning their own alternative or extended walks.

Each walk includes a "my journal" page for you to record your experiences. There are also details of how to share your interests in a particular walk and suggest a great day out.

Details of further walks along the Kent coast and across the county are available from www.kent.gov.uk/explorekent.

Please take a few minutes to complete and return the Feedback form at the end of this guidebook. Your feedback will help Kent County Council to develop its range of walking guides.

a feast of
fine architecture

Rochester, set on the banks of the River Medway, is an ideal
place to start exploring the commercial, military and historical
significance of the Saxon Shore Way.

20

© Crown copyright 100019238.

Location: Rochester

Distance: 3 miles (4.8 km)

Time: allow 1 hour 30 minutes

Explorer Map: 163

Terrain: urban pavements (take care crossing roads)

Stiles: 0

Parking: near civic centre or in public car parks

Refreshments and facilities: cafes, restaurants, public houses and bars throughout Rochester town centre

Public transport: for information about local bus and train services in Kent, contact Traveline tel: 0870 6082608, www.traveline.org.uk

Step count: approx 6000

Dog friendly

Explore Rochester Castle and Cathedral, on a delightful circular walk through this ancient town's bustling streets. Look out for the many landmark buildings made famous in the novels of Charles Dickens.

Start on the riverfront where the remains of a Roman bridge were discovered in the 19th century. Many historians believe the Romans had several bridges spanning the river here – the lowest crossing point on the Medway. Today, the river is still very important to the local economy. Admire the dramatic river views from Rochester Bridge.

A short stroll leads to the towering remains of the Norman castle. It was one of the earliest stone castles to be built in England. Remnants of the town's Roman walls can be discovered in the stonework. The castle was built by Bishop Gundulph.

Equally awe-inspiring is Rochester Cathedral. The cathedral was founded in AD 604 by Bishop Justus. It is the second oldest in England and attracts thousands of visitors and pilgrims from across the world every year. Step inside and view the Gundulph Tower and crypt – the oldest part of the cathedral.

At Crow Lane, look out for Restoration House. This is an Elizabethan red brick house where Charles II stayed in 1660. It appears as Satis House, the home of Miss Haversham in Charles Dickens' novel Great Expectations.

Follow the Saxon Shore Way along East Row, across the recreation ground to Fort Pitt Hill. Turn towards the river again, crossing New Road Avenue, and down Hammond Hill to the High Street. Piers, wharves and warehouses along the riverfront indicate the commercial importance of this waterway. Follow the High Street into Eastgate and the historic heart of Rochester.

The Guildhall, with its magnificent moulded plaster ceilings, was built in 1687. The building is now the Rochester Museum.

Nearby, The Historic Dockyard at Chatham, gives visitors a unique insight into the local importance of shipbuilding and Medway's naval connections. Visit www.chdt.org.uk for further information.

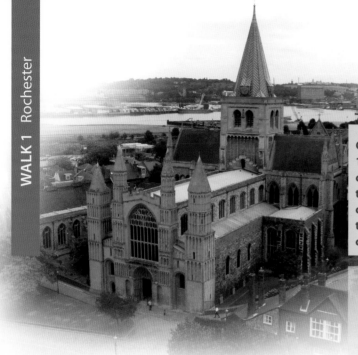

Gundulf, consecrated Bishop of Rochester in 1077, was responsible for the building of the cathedral we see today and the first stone castle to defend the town and the River Medway. The castle's towering ragstone keep, the tallest in the country, was constructed in the early 12th century.

22

look out for...

- Restoration House where Charles II stayed in 1660

- The Vines – a garden, originally a monastery vineyard, tucked away behind the cathedral

- La Providence – a square of almshouses founded to provide homes for French Protestants fleeing to England

- Roman and medieval remains of the city wall at Blue Boar Lane

- Rochester Bridge – dramatic views of the busy River Medway and beyond

did you know?

Henry VIII is believed to have met Anne of Cleves for the first time in 1540 at Old Hall, Rochester.

The Synagogue, at Ship Lane near Hammond Hill, is the only one in England with its own graveyard.

Richard Dadd, a Victorian artist known for his fairy paintings, was tried at Rochester for the murder of his father.

Fort Pitt was the site of the principal military hospital in the early 19th century and was chosen by Florence Nightingale as the first Army Medical School.

Troy Town, a small area of Rochester just 500 metres from the historic centre, is named after a wealthy Georgian wine merchant and landowner, John Cazeneuve Troy. He made his home there and attracted other successful business people to live nearby.

For more walks including accessible heritage trails, visit www.fortifications.org

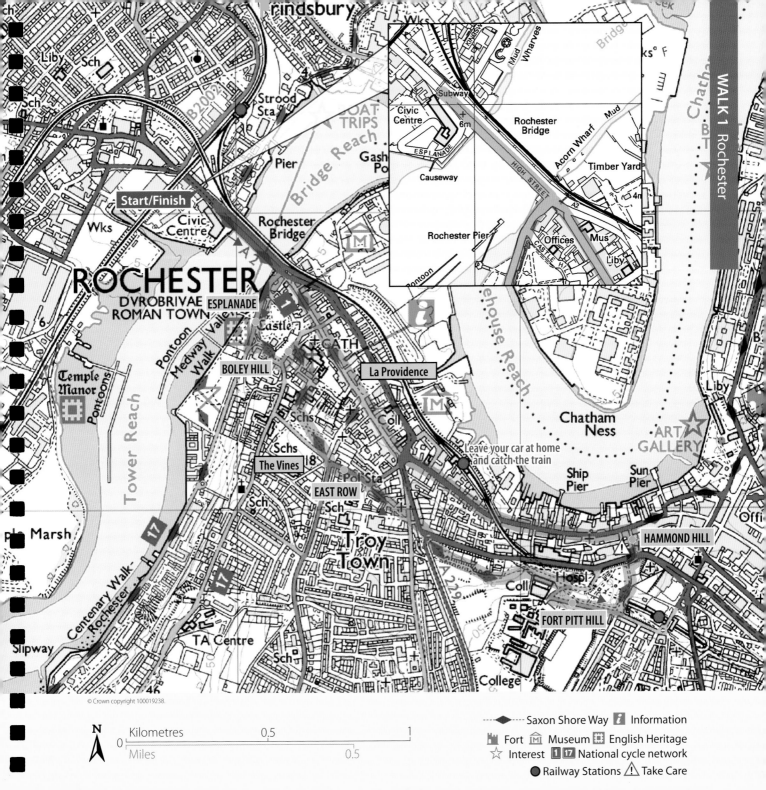

rindsbury

Liby Sch

Strood Sta.

BOAT TRIPS

Pier

Gash Po

Bridge Reach

B2002

4

Wks

Start/Finish

Civic Centre

Rochester Bridge

ROCHESTER
DVROBRIVAE **ESPLANADE**
ROMAN TOWN

Wks

A2

Castle

CATH

Pontoon

Medway Walk

Valley

BOLEY HILL

La Providence

Temple Manor

Pontoons

Tower Reach

Schs

Schs

Coll

The Vines

18

EAST ROW

Pol Sta

Sch

Sch

Marsh

17

Centenary Walk

Rochester

17

Troy Town

TA Centre

Sch

Slipway

46

© Crown copyright 100019238.

Inset map:

Wks

LONGSW

Mud

Wharves

Bridge

cks° F

Subway

Civic Centre

6m

ESPLANADE

Rochester Bridge

Acorn Wharf

Mud

HIGH STREET

Timber Yard

4n

Causeway

A2

Rochester Pier

CASTLE HILL

Offices

Mus

Liby

Right / main map continued:

Chath

B

Warehouse Reach

i

M

M

5

Chatham Ness

ART GALLERY

Leave your car at home and catch the train

Ship Pier

Sun Pier

Offi

Liby

HAMMOND HILL

Hospl

Coll

A229

Coll

FORT PITT HILL

College

Sch

50

Legend:

- - - ◆ Saxon Shore Way   **i** Information

🏰 Fort   M Museum   English Heritage

☆ Interest   **1** **17** National cycle network

● Railway Stations   ⚠ Take Care

N

0   Kilometres   0.5   1

Miles   0.5

my journal

Date..

I completed the walk in..........................hours and..........................minutes.

My highlights:

This page is for you to record your day exploring the Saxon Shore Way. You may also like to let us know about your experience along the route, recommend a walk or suggest a great day out. E-mail your comments to **explorekent@kent.gov.uk** with the subject title "the Saxon Shore Way", or post to: the Saxon Shore Way, Environment and Waste, Kent County Council, Invicta House, Maidstone, Kent ME14 1XX.

boatyards & buntings

The Swale was probably twice the width it is today in Roman times. Oare Creek has a long tradition for boatbuilding and fishing. The open marshes are an important nature reserve renowned for vast flocks of migrating birds.

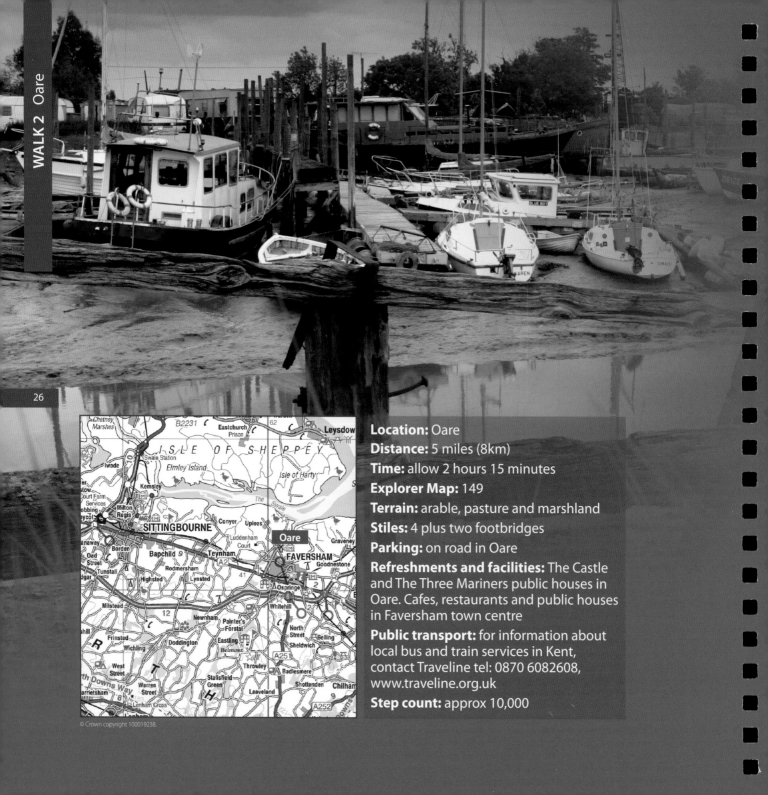

26

Location: Oare

Distance: 5 miles (8km)

Time: allow 2 hours 15 minutes

Explorer Map: 149

Terrain: arable, pasture and marshland

Stiles: 4 plus two footbridges

Parking: on road in Oare

Refreshments and facilities: The Castle and The Three Mariners public houses in Oare. Cafes, restaurants and public houses in Faversham town centre

Public transport: for information about local bus and train services in Kent, contact Traveline tel: 0870 6082608, www.traveline.org.uk

Step count: approx 10,000

© Crown copyright 100019238.

This is the coastal fringe of the Garden of England where fishing and boatbuilding have been a way of life for centuries. Other traditional industries, such as brick making and gunpowder manufacture, have also left their mark on the landscape.

From just outside Oare village, follow Oare Creek towards the sounds of the wind whipping through the rigging of the many moored boats. Take the route of the waterway past the boatyards and around the point.

There are stunning views from here overlooking the Isle of Harty and across the Greater Thames Estuary to the North Sea beyond. The walk then proceeds along the sea wall which divides the saltwater marshes from the main freshwater marshes. The wall was constructed after the Great Storm of 1953.

There is a marked difference between the plants and wildlife to be discovered on the salt marshes and the inland freshwater marshes. The freshwater marshes have been gradually reclaimed over many years. These are now managed for grazing and wildlife.

This area, Swale Site of Special Scientific Interest and Oare Marshes Nature Reserve, is internationally renowned for the thousands of migrating birds taking advantage of the marshes and rich mudflats.

For further information about the Nature Reserve, visit www.kentwildlife.org.uk

The marshes are criss-crossed by freshwater dykes and open water scrapes. Hides are dotted across the landscape for the numerous bird watchers who gather here each year.

Leaving the marshes, follow the route through classic sheep pasture towards Luddenham Court Farm and St Mary's Church. Strike off across the fields back towards Oare. At the top of the hill, before descending into the village, look back for panoramic views across The Swale to the new Isle of Sheppey bridge.

The historic town of Faversham is a short distance away – a vital link on the road between Canterbury and London in the Middle Ages. Shipbuilding, oysterbeds, fisheries and gunpowder have helped the market town to thrive. It is the home of Shepherd Neame, Britain's oldest brewers.

Imported fruit trees were planted in Kent, earning its reputation as the Garden of England, by Henry VIII's fruiterer.

28

look out for...

- St Mary's Church, Luddenham
- Birds - lapwing, teal, gadwall, coot, moorhen, snipe, reed buntings, sedge warbler
- Butterflies - red admiral, painted lady, clouded yellow
- Marsh plants - golden samphire, lesser reedmace, frogbit
- Organic butchers at Luddenham Court Farm

did you know?

The Isle of Sheppey was originally known as Sheep Isle.

The Isle of Sheppey has the largest area of wetlands in the UK.

Shepherd Neame, of Faversham, was founded in 1698 and is Britain's oldest independent brewers.

Gunpowder was manufactured in this area from the 16th century. To find out how to explore the remains visit www.gunpowderworks.co.uk

There is a 16th century Guildhall in the centre of Faversham.

James II was imprisoned in Market Street, Faversham, after a local fisherman discovered him attempting to flee to France.

Faversham's Oyster Fishery Company is believed to have been the first formally recognised company in the world and was in existence in 1189.

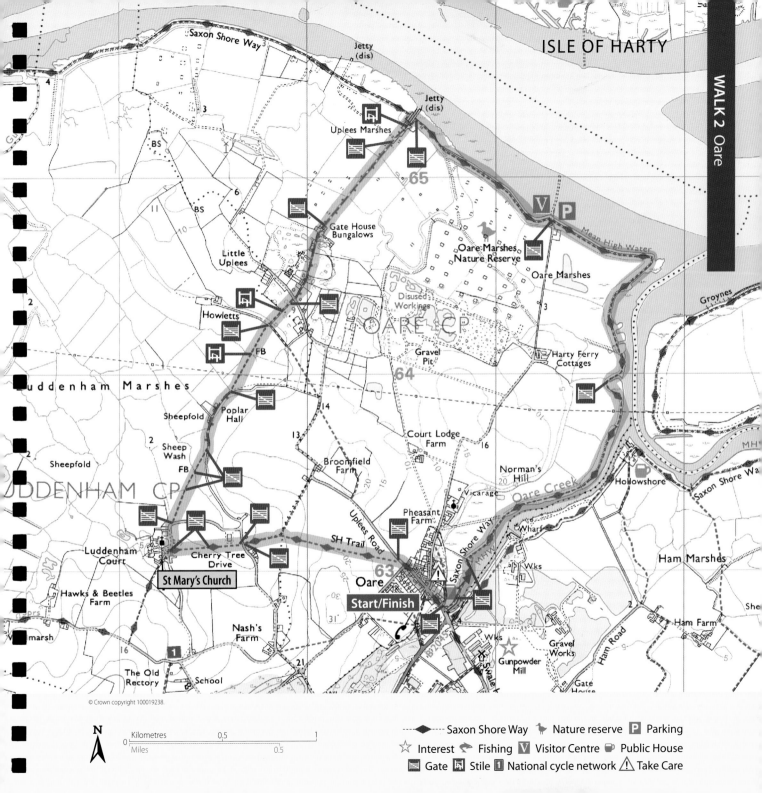

ISLE OF HARTY

Saxon Shore Way

Jetty (dis)

Jetty (dis)

Uplees Marshes

65

Gate House Bungalows

Little Uplees

Howletts

FB

Oare Marshes Nature Reserve

V **P**

Mean High Water

Oare Marshes

OARE CP

Disused Workings

Gravel Pit

64

Harty Ferry Cottages

Groynes

Luddenham Marshes

Sheepfold

Poplar Hall

Sheep Wash

FB

LUDDENHAM CP

Sheepfold

Luddenham Court

Cherry Tree Drive

St Mary's Church

Hawks & Beetles Farm

marsh

The Old Rectory

School

Nash's Farm

Broomfield Farm

Court Lodge Farm

Uplees Road

SH Trail

Norman's Hill

Vicarage

Pheasant Farm

Oare

Oare Creek

Saxon Shore Way

Hollowshore

Wharf

Saxon Shore Way

Ham Marshes

63

Start/Finish

Wks

Gunpowder Mill

Gravel Works

Ham Road

Wks

Ham Farm

She

Gate House

© Crown copyright 100019238.

N

Kilometres 0.5 1
0
Miles 0.5

- - - ◆ - - - Saxon Shore Way   🐦 Nature reserve   **P** Parking
☆ Interest   🎣 Fishing   **V** Visitor Centre   🍺 Public House
▦ Gate   🔳 Stile   **1** National cycle network   ⚠ Take Care

my journal

Date ....

I completed the walk in .... hours and .... minutes.

My highlights:

This page is for you to record your day exploring the Saxon Shore Way. You may also like to let us know about your experience along the route, recommend a walk or suggest a great day out. E-mail your comments to **explorekent@kent.gov.uk** with the subject title "the Saxon Shore Way", or post to: the Saxon Shore Way, Environment and Waste, Kent County Council, Invicta House, Maidstone, Kent ME14 1XX.

a taste of the
Garden of England

Leading through orchards and soft fruit farms –
a perfect introduction to one of the most tranquil
areas of the county.

32

© Crown copyright 100019238.

Location: Grove Ferry

Distance: 5.9 miles (9.4km)

Time: allow 2 hours 30 minutes

Explorer Map: 150

Terrain: field, orchard paths and some roadway

Stiles: 0

Parking: Grove Ferry picnic site

Refreshments and facilities: KCC picnic area and the Grove Ferry Inn public house. Public house at East Stourmouth and Plucks Gutter

Public transport: for information about local bus and train services in Kent, contact Traveline tel: 0870 6082608, www.traveline.org.uk

Step count: approx 11,800

🐾 **Dog friendly**

The Grove Ferry Inn, and its adjoining picnic park is an ideal starting point for both the circular walk through East and West Stourmouth and the linear walk to Plucks Gutter. Today's fertile fields were once under water and a ferry was needed right into the 1500s to take travellers across the waters of the Wantsum Channel.

From the car park, strike off along the path to join the banks of the Great Stour - home to many river boats and pleasure crafts offering trips. Leave the riverside and the picnic site to head towards the Little Stour.

During spring the peaceful banks of the Little Stour are lined with flowering hawthorn and cow parsley. The orchards nearby are famed for their early displays of blossom.

Wildlife, particularly birds, flourish in this area, which is set near Stodmarsh National Nature Reserve – more than 240 acres of wetlands and reedbeds. Birdsong is bound to be a feature of any walk along these picturesque paths.

Grove Ferry is known for growing fruit and vegetables. Criss-crossed by drainage ditches and dykes surrounding small villages and historic farmhouses. The tracks across this marshland are very popular with people enjoying the open landscape with long views across the fields.

The two villages on the circular route – East Stourmouth and West Stourmouth – are examples of the many small, attractive settlements to be discovered along these lanes. They retain a traditional rural atmosphere although they are just a few miles from the city of Canterbury and its historic Cathedral.

Take time to explore All Saints' Church in West Stourmouth before returning to the path and back to Grove Ferry. The church, which can claim Saxon origins, has a 17th century pulpit and a fine Royal Arms of George III.

The linear walk across the marshes from Grove Ferry to the Dog and Duck public house at Plucks Gutter is also a popular choice. It has been developed to be suitable for off-road electric scooter users.

The Little Stour and Great Stour join at Plucks Gutter and flow off to the sea at Sandwich. Look out for the old ferry cottage. The hamlet is named after a Dutch drainage engineer, Ploeg, whose grave can be seen in All Saints' Church, West Stourmouth.

Details of the linear walk are available on our website. Look for 'Walks For All 1' at www.kent.gov.uk/explorekent

Why not explore Grove Ferry by water? Take a boat trip along the River Stour.

34

look out for...

- Boats – trips available
- Orchards
- Soft fruits such as Kentish strawberries
- Arable crops
- All Saints' Church, West Stourmouth
  (The Churches Conservation Trust)
- Birds - swans, mallards, lapwing and redshank

did you know?

Lavender was once grown commercially in this area and its oils distilled at Grove Ferry. The quality of the lavender water was praised by the actress Ellen Terry.

Grove Ferry Country Park is an ideal spot for picnicing or fishing. Fishing rights were granted during the reign of Henry II and are still available today.

The marshlands at Stodmarsh were originally drained by Augustinian monks to graze their mares in foal.

Kent County Council's 'Walks for All 1' pack is available, free of charge, at www.kent.gov.uk/explorekent. The pack includes 1 mile (1.6km) and 5 mile (8km) easy access walks in Grove Ferry.

A Hurricane aircraft shot down in the Battle of Britain crashed on farmland at West Stourmouth.

All Saints' Church, West Stourmouth, is possibly the second oldest parish church in England. Its massive western brick buttresses were erected not long after an earthquake in 1579.

For information on all that is made, manufactured and grown in Kent visit www.kentishfare.co.uk

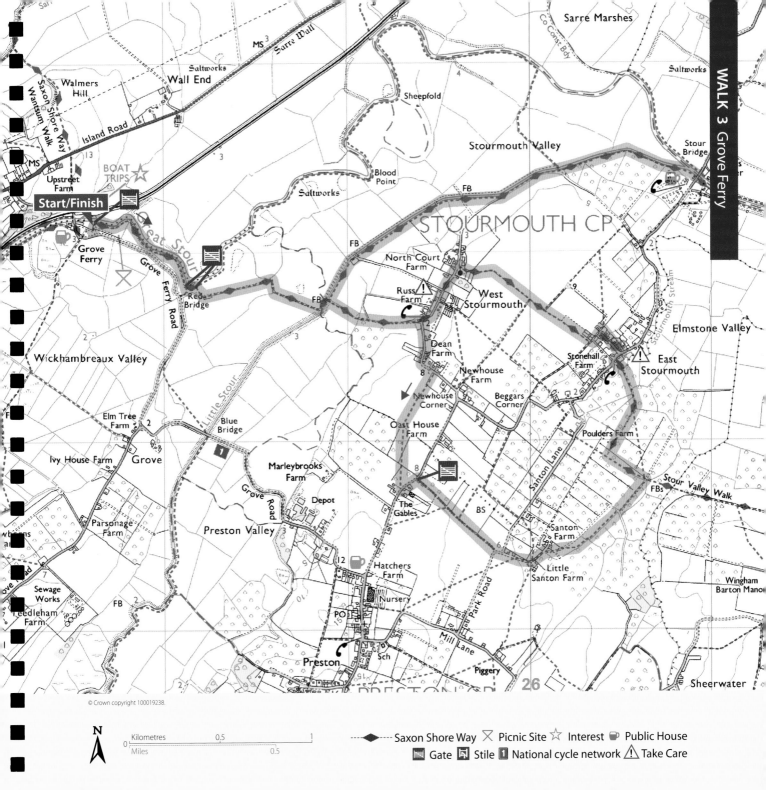

Sarre Marshes

Co Const Bdy

Saltworks

Stour Bridge

Stourmouth Valley

Saltworks

Wall End

Sheepfold

Walmers Hill

Island Road

Blood Point

FB

STOURMOUTH CP

Elmstone Valley

Saxon Wantsum Shore Way Walk

MS

Upstreet Farm

BOAT TRIPS ☆

Saltworks

North Court Farm

Start/Finish

Russ Farm !

West Stourmouth

Stonehall Farm

East Stourmouth !

Grove Ferry

Great Stour

Grove Ferry Road

Red Bridge

FB

Dean Farm

Newhouse Farm

Poulders Farm

Wickhambreaux Valley

Little Stour

Newhouse Corner

Oast House Farm

Beggars Corner

Santon Lane

FBs

Stour Valley Walk

Elm Tree Farm

Blue Bridge

1

The Gables

BS

Ivy House Farm

Grove

Marleybrooks Farm

Depot

Santon Farm

Wingham Barton Manor

Grove Road

Parsonage Farm

Preston Valley

Hatchers Farm

Little Santon Farm

Sewage Works

Teedleham Farm

FB

Nursery

PO

Park Road

Mill Lane

Sch

Preston

Piggery

Sheerwater

26

© Crown copyright 100019238.

N

Kilometres   0.5   1
Miles   0.5

◆ Saxon Shore Way ✗ Picnic Site ☆ Interest 🍺 Public House
▦ Gate 🏠 Stile **1** National cycle network ⚠ Take Care

my journal

Date..

I completed the walk in................................hours and................................minutes.

My highlights:

This page is for you to record your day exploring the Saxon Shore Way. You may also like to let us know about your experience along the route, recommend a walk or suggest a great day out. E-mail your comments to **explorekent@kent.gov.uk** with the subject title "the Saxon Shore Way", or post to: the Saxon Shore Way, Environment and Waste, Kent County Council, Invicta House, Maidstone, Kent ME14 1XX.

flights over the fairways

The busy riverside creates a lively and colourful start.
The paths quickly branch away from the riverfront to
cross the immaculate greens and fairways of a coastal
golf course and down to the shingle foreshore at
Sandwich Bay.

© Crown copyright 100019238.

Location: Sandwich

Distance: 5.1 miles (8.2km)

Time: allow 2 hours 30 minutes

Explorer Map: 150

Terrain: paths and tracks

Stiles: 6

Parking: at The Quay, Sandwich

Refreshments and facilities: public toilets at The Quay; many cafes, restaurants and public houses in Sandwich

Public transport: for information about local bus and train services in Kent, contact Traveline tel: 0870 6082608, www.traveline.org.uk

Step count: approx 10,200

Sandwich is one of the historic Cinque Ports. The town, originating in the seventh century, grew up as a trading centre and gateway to mainland Europe. The port was at its most prosperous in the 1200s. The historic quayside marks the start of this relaxing walk.

Follow the path alongside the river until it flows away to the north east and the Saxon Shore Way separates from the Stour Valley Walk. The path soon heads off across the famous Royal St George's golf course and down to the open sea at Sandwich Bay.

Enjoy the views across the bay and then follow the route back across the sand dunes and salt marshes to open fields and pastures.

The rich and varied habitats make this a particularly attractive area for enthusiasts watching many species of over-wintering and migrating birds.

The path passes by the entrance to the popular Sandwich Bay Bird Observatory Trust Field Centre. The centre is open daily and is a good source of information about wildlife in the area generally as well as rarer sightings. The observatory carries out scientific bird migration and monitoring programmes for national and international projects. From the bird observatory, the route passes through the Sandwich and Hacklinge Site of Special Scientific Interest and on through small farms and arable field.

Leave the fields and head back towards the hustle and bustle of Sandwich. Take a few minutes to explore the narrow streets and historic houses before leaving the main road. Follow the former port's ancient town wall to return to the quayside.

Guided boat trips are available from The Quay. The river tours include talks about the history of Sandwich and the local environment.

Nearby, the archaeological remains and museum at Richborough reveal the changing importance and fortunes of this part of the Kent coast in Roman Britain.

look out for...

- Sandwich Bay Bird Observatory
- Wildfowl, wading birds, visiting and resident species including mute swans, curlew, corn bunting, oyster catcher, grey heron
- Wood mouse, water vole
- Southern marsh orchid, lizard orchid
- Scarecrows in early spring
- Moths, such as elephant hawk, five spot burnet and humming bird hawk moth. Dragonflies.

Butterflies, such as red admiral, marbled white, meadow brown, painted lady and peacock.

did you know?

The Royal St George's Golf Course is one of the most famous and difficult golf courses in the world. The golf club was founded in 1887 and has played host to 13 Open Championships.

Sandwich was unusually established on a spit of sand in the seventh century and became an important port.

Henry III's sailors defeated the French in the Battle of Sandwich.

For more walks including accessible heritage trails, visit www.fortifications.org

Sandwich was one of the first towns in England to have an appointed Mayor.

Sandwich Guildhall was built in 1576 and was modified during the 20th century.

The Moot Horn, hanging in Sandwich Guildhall, was used as far back as the 12th century to summon local people to hear important announcements.

The Barbican Gate, built in the 16th century, was the former tollgate to the bridge over the River Stour.

The modern sandwich is said to have been invented by the fourth Earl of Sandwich who called for cheese, bread and meat to be served so that he could continue gambling instead of dining formally. The story goes that other players also called for the "same as Sandwich".

Map Labels

Great Stonar

Works

Swing Bridge

The Quay
T.A Centre

The Salutation

SANDWICH

Gazen Salts
Nature Reserve
Recn
Ground

PC

The King's
House

FB

Start/Finish

T.A Centre

Guildhall

White Cliffs Country Trail

Green Wall

Vigo Sprong

Little Sandown
Farm

Cemy

Town Wall
(Course of)

FB

Sch

Leave your car at home
and catch the train

Sandwich Sta

Nursery

St Bartholomew's
Hospital

Nursery

Cross

Sch

Nursery

Deal Road

MS

Coventon Lane

Worth
Hill

Links
Farm

Temptye
Farmhouse

Little
Temptye

The Delf

Brewen's
Bridge

Blue Pigeons
Farm

Fry Dike

FB

CH

Downs
Farm

Valley Walk

Sandwich Bay
Nature Reserve

PC

Royal St George's Golf Course

WORTH CP

Saxon Shore Way

CH

PC

Groyne

Old Haven

Toll

Newcut
Bridge

Guilford Road

Sandwich Bay
Estate

Sandwich Bay
Estate

Old Downs
Farm

Sandwich Bird
Observatory

Toll

Ppg Sta

BS

Little Downs
Bridge

Isle of Dogs

Dickson's
Corner

North Stream

Lyddcourt
Stile

Lydden

Mary Bax's
Stone

© Crown copyright 100019238.

Due to open
Mid 2005

N

Kilometres
0   0.5   1
Miles
0.5

Legend

◆—◆ Saxon Shore Way   🦃 Nature reserve

P Parking   ▶ Golf course   ☆ Interest   ⚲ Public House

PC Public Convenience   𝒊 Information   ▦ Gate   ⌸ Stile

① National cycle network   ● Railway Station   ⚠ Take Care

my journal

Date ....

I completed the walk in .... hours and .... minutes.

My highlights:

This page is for you to record your day exploring the Saxon Shore Way. You may also like to let us know about your experience along the route, recommend a walk or suggest a great day out. E-mail your comments to **explorekent@kent.gov.uk** with the subject title "the Saxon Shore Way", or post to: the Saxon Shore Way, Environment and Waste, Kent County Council, Invicta House, Maidstone, Kent ME14 1XX.

guarding the gateway

If Kent can be characterised as England's frontline county, then nowhere does the "front" come closer to the surface than at St Margaret's Bay.

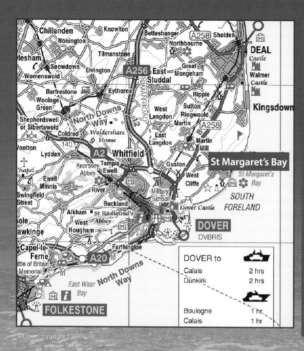

© Crown copyright 100049298

44

Location: St Margaret's Bay

Distance: 4.7 miles (7.5km)

Time: allow 2 hours 45 minutes

Explorer Map: 138

Stiles: 1

Parking: car park at St Margaret's Bay

Refreshments and facilities: the Coastguard public house and public toilets at St Margaret's beach; tearooms at former Coastguard Station, at the top of the Leas.

Public transport: for information about local bus and train services in Kent, contact Traveline tel: 0870 6082608, www.traveline.org.uk

Step count: approx 9,400

This circular walk, much of it along quiet roads where the going is very easy, is dotted with reminders of Britain's more recent conflicts. The views from the cliff tops of the South Foreland and The Leas, above the Bay, are a reminder of the strategic and economic importance of this busy seaway. The coast of France can be seen across the Channel on a clear day.

From the car park, walk past the Coastguard public house and back up Bay Hill. Bear left to follow the Saxon Shore Way signs along Beach Road past the popular Pines Gardens and St. Margaret's Museum.

The centrepiece of the Pines Gardens is a brooding statue of Winston Churchill – a reminder in bronze of Britain's darkest days when Nazi invaders were just 20 miles (32km) away. The entrance to the St Margaret's Museum is dramatically guarded by two naval cannons.

The path then leads through Lighthouse Down and past the whitewashed South Foreland Lighthouse. The striking Victorian lighthouse is now conserved by the National Trust. The concrete remnants of cross-Channel gun positions and observation posts are still clearly visible in the undergrowth.

Once past the lighthouse, follow the track along Lighthouse Road towards the village of St Margaret's at Cliffe. Cross the main road and continue along The Droveway to pick up the footpath heading across fields towards the Free Down.

At the bottom of the valley, the route passes through the middle of the former gun position of a high velocity howitzer "Bruce".

Follow the path uphill again on to The Leas where the former Coastguard Station has been converted into a welcoming tearoom with excellent Channel views.

Continue along the clifftops where the underground military defences are now securely barred to keep people out. This is a good place to look for the tracks and burrows of foxes, badgers and rabbits.

At the end of the walk, the shingle beach of St Margaret's Bay, toilet facilities, The Coastguard public house and car parking, are just a five-minute downhill stroll.

The White Cliffs Countryside Project was set up to help conserve and enhance the special coast and countryside of Dover and Shepway districts, and make it accessible to all.
(www.whitecliffscountryside.org.uk)

look out for...

- The Pines Gardens
- Statue of Winston Churchill
- St Margaret's Museum
- South Foreland Lighthouse – National Trust
- Ship Spotters
- Cross-Channel gun positions from the Second World War - called Winnie & Pooh
- Views of the White Cliffs and the French coast

The Romans placed two lighthouses, known as pharos, to alert seafarers in the treacherous Dover Straits. One was built at nearby Dover Castle and a second on the Western Heights.

did you know?

Marconi conducted experiments in radio communication at South Foreland lighthouse.

St Margaret's Bay was a regular landing point for smugglers in East Kent.

St Margaret's smock windmill was constructed in 1928 to generate power.

Dover Patrol Memorial, an impressive needle memorial on The Leas, commemorates the heroism of the Royal Navy's Dover Patrol in two World Wars.

Both playwright Noel Coward and author Ian Fleming – creator of James Bond – made their home at St Margaret's Bay.

46

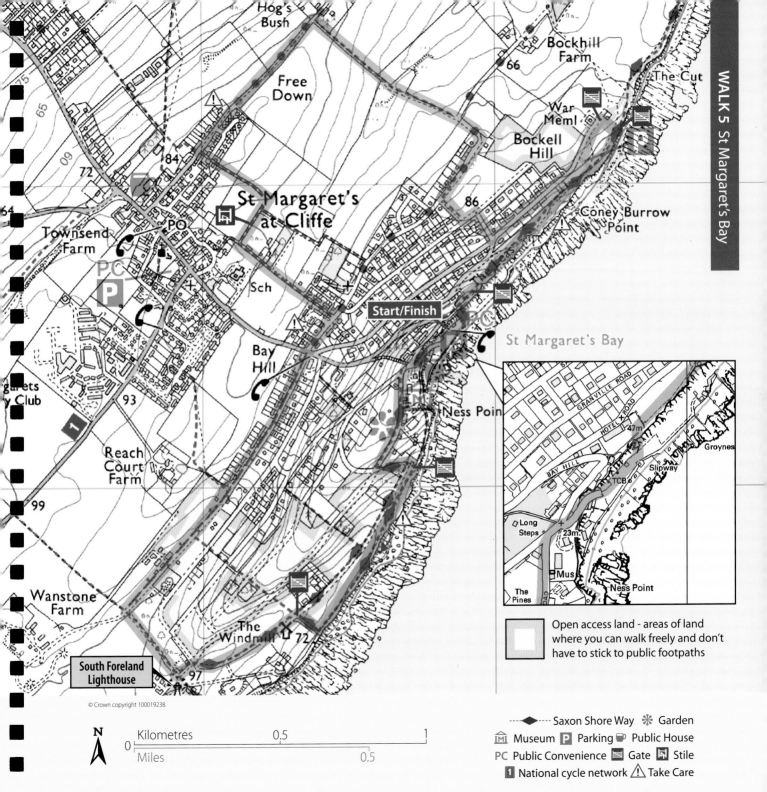

Hog's Bush

Bockhill Farm

The Cut

Free Down

66

War Meml

Bockell Hill

86

Coney Burrow Point

St Margaret's at Cliffe

84

72

PO

PC P

Townsend Farm

Sch

Start/Finish

PC

St Margaret's Bay

Bay Hill

margarets y Club

93

Ness Point

Reach Court Farm

99

The Windmill 72

Wanstone Farm

97

South Foreland Lighthouse

© Crown copyright 100019238.

GRANVILLE ROAD

HOTEL X ROAD

47m

Groynes

BAY HILL

Slipway

TCB

Long Steps

23m

Mus

The Pines

Ness Point

Open access land - areas of land where you can walk freely and don't have to stick to public footpaths

N

Kilometres
0   0.5   1
Miles
0   0.5

----◆---- Saxon Shore Way   ✳ Garden
🏛 Museum   🅿 Parking   ⌐ Public House
PC Public Convenience   ▦ Gate   ▣ Stile
1 National cycle network   ⚠ Take Care

my journal

Date...

I completed the walk in.............................hours and.............................minutes.

My highlights:

This page is for you to record your day exploring the Saxon Shore Way. You may also like to let us know about your experience along the route, recommend a walk or suggest a great day out. E-mail your comments to **explorekent@kent.gov.uk** with the subject title "the Saxon Shore Way", or post to: the Saxon Shore Way, Environment and Waste, Kent County Council, Invicta House, Maidstone, Kent ME14 1XX.

a Kentish safari

Discover elephants, giraffes, hyenas
and bison...

© Crown copyright 100019238.

Location: Lympne

Distance: 2.7 miles (4.3km)

Time: allow 1 hour 45 minutes

Explorer Map: 138

Terrain: tracks and paths. Very steep in places

Stiles: 0

Parking: in village centre

Refreshments and facilities: County Members public house, Lympne

Public transport: for information about local bus and train services in Kent, contact Traveline tel: 0870 6082608, www.traveline.org.uk

Step count: approx 5,400

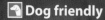 **Dog friendly**

This circular walk passes alongside the grounds of Port Lympne Wild Animal Park, owned by The John Aspinall Foundation, which is home to 500 animals representing 50 species.

From the village of Lympne, cross over Roman Road and follow the footpath signs past historic Lympne Castle. Take the path down the former cliff, passing Lympne Place, and on to the remains of Stutfall Castle – Portus Lemanis, the former Roman fort.

Portus Lemanis was built to protect the fleet. It was the site of the fourth Saxon Shore fort taking advantage of a natural haven and key routes to Canterbury and London. This is where the River Rother met the sea in Roman times.

After the Norman Invasion, the Roman fort was left to decay. Lympne Castle was built at the top of the cliff overlooking the marshes. Stone from the Roman fort was used in the construction of the castellated mansion.

It is also thought that there was once a Roman watchtower on or very close to where the castle stands today. And the dramatic views across the marshes and waterways make it clear why this was considered such a strategically important position.

From Stutfall Castle, follow along the peaceful banks of the Royal Military Canal – itself a fortification built to protect against any invasions during the Napoleonic Wars – skirting the foot of the former cliff line through tranquil woodland. A concrete pillbox stands as a reminder of more recent military threats to the Kent coastline.

Follow the path back up the cliffs. From here, animals, such as giraffes, from Port Lympne Wild Animal Park, can be spotted enjoying the Kent countryside.

As the walk reaches the summit of the cliffs to rejoin the road, the marsh opens up behind with breathtaking views over the reclaimed lands and beyond to the open sea.

Excellent sightlines were essential for the security of the country. Panoramic views were also important for the many Romney Marsh smugglers and the excise officers striving to catch up with them.

look out for...

- **Remains of the Roman fort – Stutfall Castle**
- **Animals at Port Lympne Park**
- **Royal Military Canal**
- **World War II pillbox**
- **Lympne Castle and tower**
- **Blackberries in late summer**
- **Stunning views of the sea from the Saxon Shore Way near Lympne Castle**

52

The mansion at Port Lympne Park was built for Sir Philip Sassoon during World War I.

did you know?

Port Lympne Wild Animal Park contains the world's largest family gorilla house and the world's largest captive breeding herd of black rhino outside Africa.

The Royal Military Canal stretches for 28 miles from Hythe to Cliff End.

The name Lympne comes from the Celtic name for the River Rother, the Limen, which meant elm.

Lympne Castle was originally home to Archdeacons of Canterbury, including Thomas Becket.

Romney Marsh smugglers became particularly sophisticated at smuggling wool (owling) – an offence punishable by death.

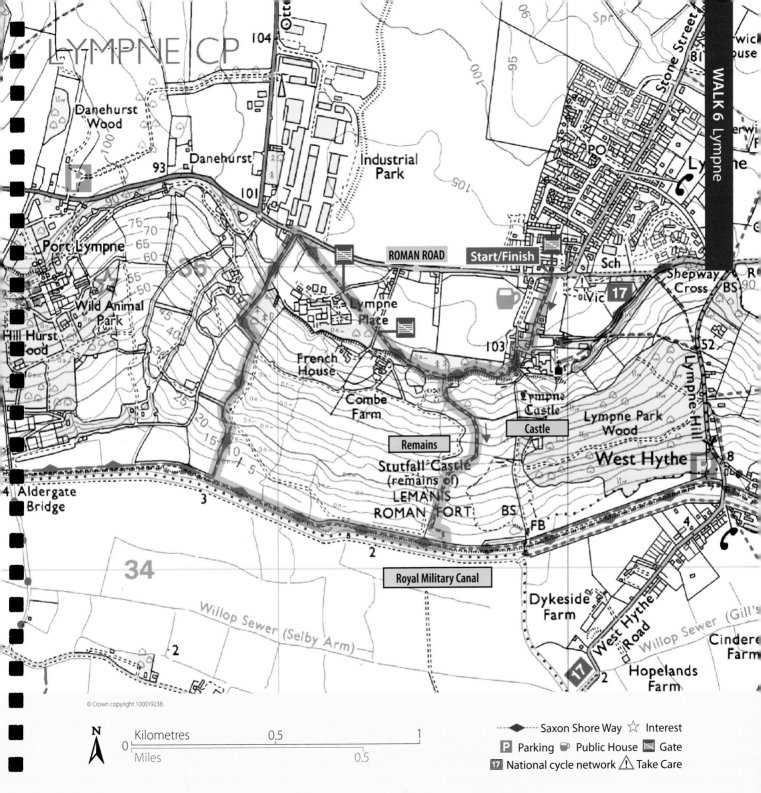

LYMPNE CP

Danehurst Wood

Danehurst

93

101

104

Ott

Industrial Park

PO

Lympne

Sch

105

100

95

Port Lympne

75
70
65
60
55
50
45
40
35
30
25
20
15
10
5

35

ROMAN ROAD

Start/Finish

Wild Animal Park

Hill Hurst Wood

Lympne Place

French House

Combe Farm

103

Vic

17

Shepway Cross

BS

52

Lympne Castle

Castle

Lympne Park Wood

Lympne Hill

West Hythe

8

P

Remains

Stutfall Castle (remains of)
LEMANIS ROMAN FORT

BS

FB

4 Aldergate Bridge

3

2

Royal Military Canal

34

Willop Sewer (Selby Arm)

2

© Crown copyright 100019238.

Dykeside Farm

West Hythe Road

Willop Sewer (Gill's

17

2

Hopelands Farm

Cinder Farm

N

Kilometres
0   0.5   1

Miles
                                                                          0.5

Saxon Shore Way   ☆ Interest
P Parking   🍺 Public House   ▦ Gate
17 National cycle network   ⚠ Take Care

my journal

Date..

I completed the walk in......................hours and......................minutes.

My highlights:

This page is for you to record your day exploring the Saxon Shore Way. You may also like to let us know about your experience along the route, recommend a walk or suggest a great day out. E-mail your comments to **explorekent@kent.gov.uk** with the subject title "the Saxon Shore Way", or post to: the Saxon Shore Way, Environment and Waste, Kent County Council, Invicta House, Maidstone, Kent ME14 1XX.

55

a natural haven

At Hamstreet Woods, the Saxon Shore Way passes
through ancient woodland along clay cliffs – now more
than six miles (9.6km) from the sea.

56

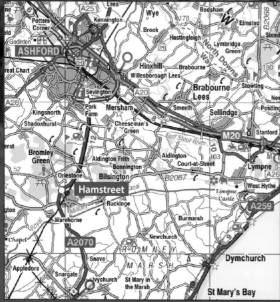

© Crown copyright 100019238.

Location: Hamstreet
Distance: 2.3 miles (3.7km)
Time: allow 1 hour 15 minutes
Explorer Map: 125
Terrain: well-defined tracks
Stiles: 0
Parking: at start of walk or on road
Refreshments and facilities: The Duke's Head public house in the village and local shops
Public transport: for information about local bus and train services in Kent, contact Traveline tel: 0870 6082608, www.traveline.org.uk
Step count: approx 4,600

🐾 **Dog friendly**

This peaceful circular walk starts and finishes at Hamstreet railway station, passing through the woodland of Hamstreet Woods National Nature Reserve. The route traces the ancient cliff line above Romney Marsh and joins the start of another popular long distance walking route – The Greensand Way.

From the station, take the footpath to the entrance of Hamstreet Woods. Follow the broad path uphill through the nature reserve along the former coastline.

English Nature uses traditional woodland management methods, such as coppicing, to encourage wildlife to flourish. Wild service (chequer) trees can be found among the oak, silver birch and hornbeam. This type of woodland flourished after the Ice Age and once covered the whole of the Weald.

The woodland glades are carpeted with bluebells and wood anemones in spring. Wild honeysuckle is also well established.

Nightingales are heard in spring and tawny owls in autumn. Other birds regularly seen include treecreeper, hawfinch and spotted flycatcher.

A large number of rare invertebrates can be found, particularly near or on decaying wood. This is a site for seeking out moths and butterflies.

Turn south and join the Greensand Way for a short distance before following the route back towards Hamstreet village. The Greensand Way starts in Hamstreet. The popular walking route runs 105 miles (169km) to Haslemere, Surrey, along a sandstone ridge through the Kent Downs and the Surrey Hills. Take time to enjoy stunning views across the marshes and rich farmland to the Royal Military Canal and beyond.

Hamstreet has been described as the "gateway to Romney Marsh". It was one of the first areas in the country to be mapped by the Ordnance Survey. Hamstreet Woods was one of the first sites in the country to be designated a National Nature Reserve.

look out for...

- Trees – oak, hornbeam, wild service
- Wildflowers – such as honeysuckle and bluebells
- Animals – squirrels, rabbits
- Butterflies and moths
- Birds – including nightingale and owl

Coppicing – cutting down trees to produce new growth – has been a sustainable way of harvesting wood for thousands of years. Coppicing allows light through to the woodland floor so bluebells and other wildflowers can flourish.

58

did you know?

Kent County Council's Walks for All 2 pack is available, free of charge, at www.kent.gov.uk/explorekent. The pack includes a 0.45 mile (0.7km) easy access walk through Hamstreet Woods.

Writers who have known Hamstreet well include: H E Bates, Noel Coward and Joseph Conrad.

The village name combines the Saxon words "ham" meaning clustered settlement and "street" meaning road.

The village centre was originally in Orlestone. People moved to Hamstreet to be closer to a source of clean spring water during the Plague.

Hamstreet is twinned with the village of Therouanne, near St Omer, in northern France.

Hamstreet is renowned for its annual fireworks displays and its summer Country Fayre.

A map of Hamstreet village appeared on a special edition set of postage stamps in 1991 to mark the bicentenary of the Ordnance Survey.

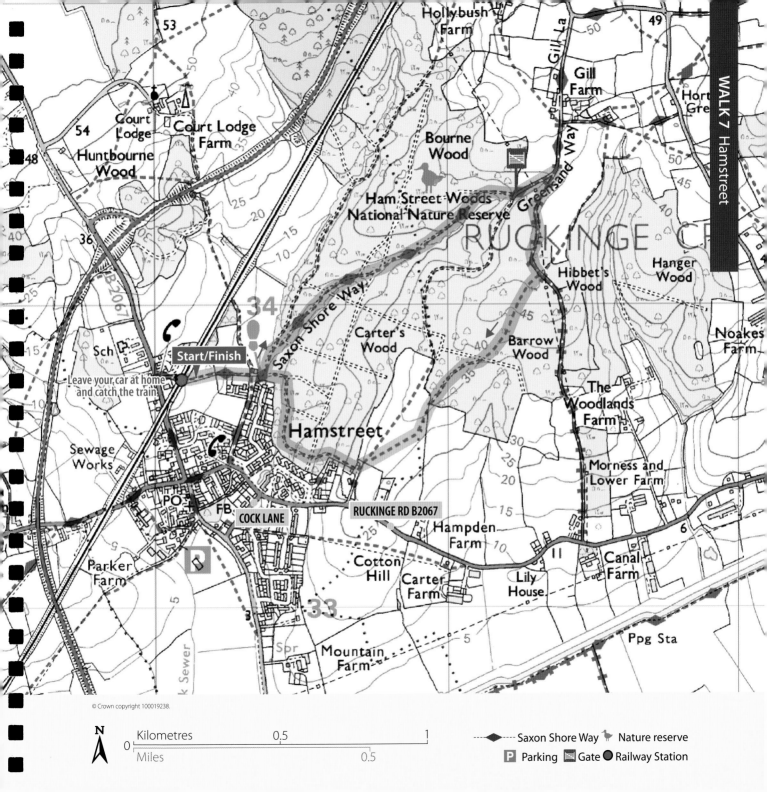

Hollybush Farm

Gill La

53

50

49

Court Lodge

Court Lodge Farm

54

Huntbourne Wood

48

36

B2067

Gill Farm

Hort Gre

Bourne Wood

Greensand Way

RUCKINGE CE

Ham Street Woods National Nature Reserve

Hibbet's Wood

Hanger Wood

34

Saxon Shore Way

Carter's Wood

Barrow Wood

Noakes Farm

Start/Finish

Leave your car at home and catch the train

Sch

The Woodlands Farm

Hamstreet

Sewage Works

Morness and Lower Farm

PO

FB

COCK LANE

RUCKINGE RD B2067

Hampden Farm

6

Parker Farm

Cotton Hill

Carter Farm

Lily House

Canal Farm

33

Mountain Farm

Ppg Sta

k Sewer

Spr

N

Kilometres
0   0.5   1

Miles
0   0.5

◆---- Saxon Shore Way   Nature reserve
P Parking   Gate   ● Railway Station

my journal

Date..

I completed the walk in.............................hours and...............................minutes.

My highlights:

This page is for you to record your day exploring the Saxon Shore Way. You may also like to let us know about your experience along the route, recommend a walk or suggest a great day out. E-mail your comments to **explorekent@kent.gov.uk** with the subject title "the Saxon Shore Way", or post to: the Saxon Shore Way, Environment and Waste, Kent County Council, Invicta House, Maidstone, Kent ME14 1XX.

relax under wide skies

Savour the atmosphere and sense of remoteness to be enjoyed on Romney Marsh throughout the year.

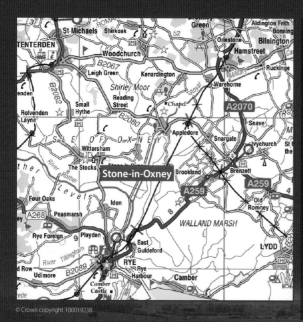

© Crown copyright 100019238.

Location: Stone-in-Oxney

Distance: 3.2 miles (5.1km)

Time: allow 2 hours

Explorer Map: 125

Terrain: rough grazing pasture, slopes and some roadway

Stiles: 11

Parking: on road at Stone-in-Oxney

Refreshments and facilities: public house in Stone-in-Oxney and neighbouring villages

Public transport: for information about local bus and train services in Kent, contact Traveline tel: 0870 6082608, www.traveline.org.uk

Step count: approx 6,400

Wide skies and the unusual quality of the light enhance panoramic and dramatic views over the Rother Levels. This is a tranquil and relaxing walk heading over the cliffs which once marked the edge of the sea and on to classic Romney Marsh sheep farming pasture.

From Stone-in-Oxney village, head to the picturesque 15th century St Mary's Church. Continue up Church Hill before branching off onto farmland and the top of Stone Cliff (54m/150ft above sea level).

Wildlife thrives in the many ditches draining this rich arable land. Before crossing the Kent Ditch – the boundary between the counties of Kent and East Sussex – look back to see hedgerows lining the ancient cliffs like soldiers on guard.

The route follows along the banks of the Royal Military Canal, a major fortification designed to keep Napoleon's forces at bay. The historic canal is a Scheduled Monument. It now plays an important role in keeping the marshes drained and is very popular locally for fishing.

Leave the banks of the canal at Stone Bridge and turn back uphill, heading across the fields to return to St Mary's.

This walk offers plenty of opportunities to discover the less familiar plants, animals and insects thriving on this large area of reclaimed land and along the banks of the canal.

Few walkers will leave the waterside without spotting a mute swan, moorhen or grey heron. Kingfishers are regularly seen in summer as are dragonflies.

However, not all the most widespread species to be discovered on the marsh are native. For example, the marsh frog, frequently called the "laughing frog" because of its rather unusual "croak", can be found right across Romney Marsh. Today's population came from just 12 Hungarian frogs introduced to a garden pond in Stone-in-Oxney in 1932. The frogs escaped on to the marsh and have flourished ever since.

Full details of all the work being done to protect and preserve the wildlife that thrives on Romney Marsh can be found at the website of the Romney Marsh Countryside Project (www.rmcp.co.uk).

63

look out for...

- **15th century St Mary's Church**
- **Royal Military Canal**
- **Water voles** (*Ratty from Kenneth Graeme's Wind in the Willows*) **and marsh frogs; mute swans, grey herons, moorhens, kingfishers; damselflies and dragonflies**
- **Yellow flag iris and fringed water lilies**
- **World War II pillbox**

"Laughing" frogs have flourished on Romney Marsh since they were first introduced in 1932.

64

did you know?

The Roman ragstone altar at St Mary's Church, Stone-in-Oxney, features carvings of Mithras the Bull.

Wealthy landowners employed "lookers" to care for their flocks of sheep grazing on Romney Marsh. Lookers huts, small brick-built houses with tiled roofs and a single chimney, were used by shepherds across the marsh from the 18th century.

The Kent Ditch is the boundary between the counties of Kent and East Sussex.

The Royal Military Canal and the Caledonian Canal are the only two wholly state-funded canals to have been built in Britain. Today, the Royal Military Canal is important for draining the marshes.

Appledore was originally a port on the estuary of the River Rother. The village now stands more than eight miles (12.8km) from the sea.

Romney Marsh provides the setting for author Russell Thorndyke's popular character Dr Syn – a vicar by day and a hard-hearted smuggler by night.

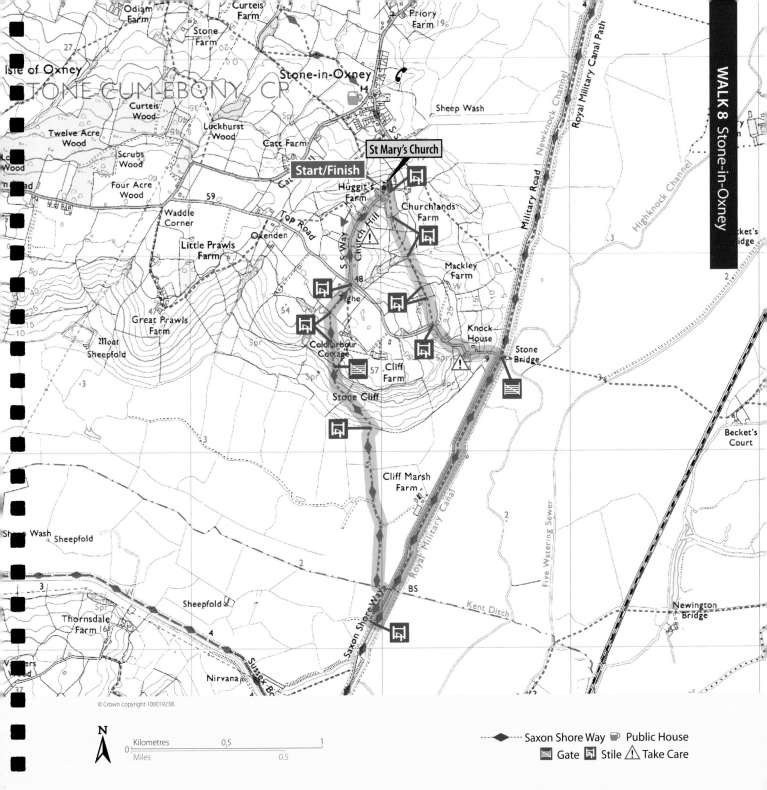

Isle of Oxney

STONE-CUM-EBONY CP

Odiam Farm

Curteis Farm

Stone Farm

Priory Farm

Stone-in-Oxney

Curteis Wood

Luckhurst Wood

Catt Farm

Sheep Wash

Twelve Acre Wood

Scrubs Wood

Four Acre Wood

Waddle Corner

Little Prawls Farm

Oxenden

Great Prawls Farm

Moat Sheepfold

St Mary's Church

Start/Finish

Huggit's Farm

Churchlands Farm

Mackley Farm

Knock House

Colharbour Cottage

Cliff Farm

Stone Cliff

Stone Bridge

Cliff Marsh Farm

Becket's Court

Shore Wash Sheepfold

Sheepfold

Thornsdale Farm

Nirvana

Newington Bridge

Newknock Channel

Royal Military Canal Path

Military Road

Highknock Channel

Royal Military Canal

Five Watering Sewer

Kent Ditch

Saxon Shore Way

Sussex Bo

BS

© Crown copyright 100019238.

N

◆ Saxon Shore Way   🍺 Public House
🏠 Gate   🚪 Stile   ⚠ Take Care

my journal

Date.................................

I completed the walk in......................hours and.......................minutes.

My highlights:

This page is for you to record your day exploring the Saxon Shore Way. You may also like to let us know about your experience along the route, recommend a walk or suggest a great day out. E-mail your comments to **explorekent@kent.gov.uk** with the subject title "the Saxon Shore Way", or post to: the Saxon Shore Way, Environment and Waste, Kent County Council, Invicta House, Maidstone, Kent ME14 1XX.

Special attractions
along or near the Saxon Shore Way circular walks

WALK 1
The Historic Dockyard Chatham
tel: **+44 (0)1634 823800**
www.chdt.org.uk

The Guildhall Museum, Rochester
Open: *daily 10am – 4.30pm*
tel: **+44 (0)1634 848717**
email: **guildhall.museum@medway.gov.uk**
**www.medway.gov.uk/index/leisure/
museums**

WALK 2
Oare Gunpowder Works
Open: *9am – 5pm weekdays, 10am
– 4pm weekends*
Visitor centre: *weekends only April
– November, 10.30am – 4.30pm*
tel: **+44 (0)1795 417850**
email: **countryparks@swale.gov.uk**
www.gunpowderworks.co.uk

Brogdale
National Fruit Collections
Open daily: *summer 10am – 5pm;
winter 10am – 4.30pm*
tel: **+44 (0)1795 535286**
email: **info@brogdale.org**
www.brogdale.org

WALK 3
Stodmarsh National Nature Reserve
English Nature Kent team
tel: **+44 (0)1233 812525**
email: **kent@english-nature.org.uk**
www.english-nature.org.uk

Sarre Windmill *(working with tours
and tearooms)*
Canterbury Road, Sarre
Open: *10am – 5pm (summer) 10am–
4pm (winter). Closed Mondays*
tel: **+44 (0)1843 847 573**

WALK 4
Sandwich Bay Bird Observatory
Open: *10am – 4pm daily*
tel: **+44 (0)1304 617341**
email: **sbbot@talk21.com**
www.sbbo.co.uk

Sandwich Guildhall Museum
Open: *April 1 – November 30 (except
Mondays)*
tel: **+44 (0)1304 617197**
www.sandwichtowncouncil.co.uk

WALK 5
South Foreland Lighthouse
Open: *April – October*
tel: **+44 (0)1304 852463** *(lighthouse)*
tel: **+44 (0)1304 202756** *(White Cliffs
Visitor Centre)*
email: **southforeland@nationaltrust.org.uk**
www.nationaltrust.org.uk

St Margaret's Museum
Open: *Easter, May Bank Holidays
and daily from end of May until
early September (closed Mondays &
Tuesdays)*
tel: **+44 (0)1304 851737**
email: **enquiries@baytrust.org.uk**
www.baytrust.org.uk

WALK 6
Port Lympne Wild Animal Park
Open: *Every day from 10am
Closed December 25*
www.totallywild.net

Romney Hythe and Dymchurch
Railway
Limited service during winter
tel: +44 (0)1797 362353
www.rhdr.org.uk

67

WALK 7

Hamstreet Woods
National Nature Reserve
English Nature Kent team
tel: **+44 (0)1233 812525**
email: **kent@english-nature.org.uk**
www.english-nature.org.uk

Rare Breeds Centre, Woodchurch
Open: *daily 10.30am – 5.30pm (April – September); Tuesday – Sunday 10.30am – 4.30pm (October – March)*
tel: **+44 (0)1233 861 493**
email: **visit@rarebreeds.org.uk**
www.rarebreeds.org.uk

WALK 8

Rye Castle Museum
Open: *limited hours closed Tuesday and Wednesday during summer; weekends only November 1 – March 31*
tel: **+44 (0)1797 226 728**
www.rye.org.uk

Kent & East Sussex Railway
Tenterden – Northiam – Bodiam
tel: **0870 060 060 74**
email: **enquiries@kesr.org.uk**
www.kesr.org.uk

KENT VISITOR INFORMATION CENTRES

Ashford: tel: +44 (0)1233 629165
email: tourism@ashford.gov.uk
www.ashford.gov.uk

Broadstairs: tel: 0870 2646111
email: tourism@thanet.gov.uk
www.tourism.thanet.gov.uk

Canterbury: tel: +44 (0)1227 378100
email: canterburyinformation@canterbury.gov.uk
www.canterbury.gov.uk

Deal: tel: +44 (0)1304 369576
email: info@deal.gov.uk
www.whitecliffscountry.org.uk

Dover: tel: +44 (0)1304 205108
email: tic@doveruk.com
www.whitecliffscountry.org.uk

Faversham: tel: +44 (0)1795 534542
email: faversham@btinternet.com
www.faversham.org.uk

Folkestone: tel: +44 (0)1303 258594
email: discoverfolkestone@btconnect.com
www.discoverfolkestone.co.uk

Gravesend: tel: +44 (0)1474 337600
email: info@towncentric.co.uk, www.towncentric.co.uk

Herne Bay: tel: +44 (0)1227 361911
email: hernebayinformation@canterbury.co.uk,
www.visithernebay.co.uk

Maidstone: tel: +44 (0)1622 602169
email: tourism@maidstone.gov.uk
www.tour-maidstone.com

Margate: tel: 0870 2646111,
email: tourism@thanet.gov.uk
www.tourism.thanet.gov.uk

New Romney: tel: +44 (0)1797 362353

email: info@discoverfolkestone.co.uk
www.discoverfolkestone.co.uk

Ramsgate: tel: 0870 2646111
email: tourism@thanet.gov.uk
www.tourism.thanet.gov.uk

Rochester: tel: +44 (0)1634 843666
email: visitor.centre@medway.gov.uk
www.medway.gov.uk

Sandwich: *(summer only)*
tel: +44 (0)1304 613565 email:
info@ticsandwich.wanadoo.co.uk
www.open-sandwich.co.uk

Sevenoaks: tel: +44 (0)1732 450305
email: tic@sevenoakstown.gov.uk
www.heartofkent.org.uk

Swanley: tel: +44 (0)1322 614660
email: tourisminfo@swanley.org.uk

Tenterden: *(summer only)*
tel: +44 (0)1580 763572
email: tenttic@ashford.gov.uk
www.ashford.gov.uk

Tonbridge: tel: +44 (0)1732 770929
email: tonbridge.castle@tmbc.gov.uk
www.tmbc.gov.uk

Tunbridge Wells: tel: +44 (0)1892 515675, email: touristinformationcentre@tunbridgewells.gov.uk
www.visittunbridgewells.com

Whitstable: tel: +44 (0)1227 275482
email: whitstableinformation@canterbury.gov.uk
www.visitwhitstable.co.uk

To order a free copy of the Kent Visitor Guide tel: **0906 294 1191** or visit: **www.kenttourism.co.uk**

68

Your Feedback

Thank you for buying Kent County Council's Saxon Shore Way guidebook. We hope you enjoy reading it and have fun exploring the coastline as it stood many centuries ago. We really appreciate feedback from our customers and use it to develop the right services and products for you. Please take a few minutes to complete and return this form.

How did you find out about the Saxon Shore Way guidebook?

☐ Explore Kent website

☐ "word of mouth"

☐ browsing in a shop

☐ Visitor Information Centre

Other

Were you given the guidebook as a gift or did you buy it?

Where did you buy your copy of this guidebook?

What do you like most about this guidebook?

What do you like least about this guidebook?

How would you rate the guidebook between 1
1 (poor) - 5 (excellent)

☐ ☐ ☐ ☐ ☐
1　2　3　4　5

About you

☐ Male　☐ Female

Age

☐ under 18 years

☐ 18 - 29

☐ 30 - 39

☐ 40 - 49

☐ 50 - 59

☐ 60 - 69

☐ Over 69

Are you a visitor or resident of Kent?

☐ Visitor　☐ Resident

Any further comments

Please tear out and send your feedback to:-
Environment and Waste, Kent County Council,
Invicta House, Maidstone, Kent ME14 1XX

Thank you for your time.
If you would like to be kept up to date with Explore Kent products please tick the box and write your name and address or your email address below. ☐

🔒 We'd like to keep you posted on Explore Kent news. Don't worry, we will not overload you with post or emails and we will not pass on or sell any personal information you share with us.

C000175315

Cycle

TOURS

Around Birmingham

Mike Ginger, Rob Green
and Gordon Selway

First published in 2002 by
Philip's, a division of
Octopus Publishing Group Ltd
2-4 Heron Quays
London E14 4JP

First edition 2002
First impression 2002

Based on the original Ordnance Survey Cycle Tours series
first published by Philip's and Ordnance Survey®.

ISBN 0-540-08202-3

The route maps in this book are reproduced from
Ordnance Survey® Landranger® mapping.

Text and compilation copyright © Philip's 2002

This product includes mapping data licensed from Ordnance
Survey® with the permission of the Controller of Her Majesty's
Stationery Office. © Crown copyright 2002. All rights reserved.
Licence number 100011710

Photographic acknowledgements

AA Photo Library 52, 77, 101 • Heart of England Tourist Board
107 • WM Chambers 11, 65, 71, 89 • Judy Todd 35, 83, 95

Contents